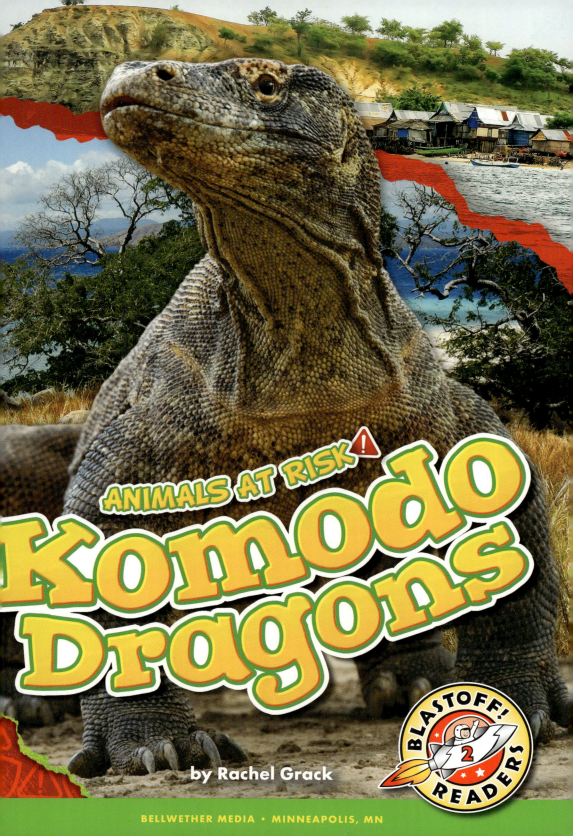

Blastoff! Readers are carefully developed by literacy experts to build reading stamina and move students toward fluency by combining standards-based content with developmentally appropriate text.

LEVELS

Level 1 provides the most support through repetition of high-frequency words, light text, predictable sentence patterns, and strong visual support.

Level 2 offers early readers a bit more challenge through varied sentences, increased text load, and text-supportive special features.

Level 3 advances early-fluent readers toward fluency through increased text load, less reliance on photos, advancing concepts, longer sentences, and more complex special features.

★ **Blastoff! Universe**

Reading Level

Grade K

Grades 1–3

Grade 4

This edition first published in 2024 by Bellwether Media, Inc.

No part of this publication may be reproduced in whole or in part without written permission of the publisher. For information regarding permission, write to Bellwether Media, Inc., Attention: Permissions Department, 6012 Blue Circle Drive, Minnetonka, MN 55343.

Library of Congress Cataloging-in-Publication Data

Names: Koestler-Grack, Rachel A., 1973- author.
Title: Komodo dragons / by Rachel Grack.
Description: Minneapolis, MN : Bellwether Media, [2024] | Series: Animals at risk | Includes bibliographical references and index. | Audience: Ages 5-8 | Audience: Grades 2-3 | Summary: "Relevant images match informative text in this introduction to Komodo dragons. Intended for students in kindergarten through third grade" Provided by publisher.
Identifiers: LCCN 2023036151 (print) | LCCN 2023036152 (ebook) | ISBN 9798886877885 (library binding) | ISBN 9798886878820 (ebook)
Subjects: LCSH: Komodo dragon--Juvenile literature.
Classification: LCC QL666.L29 K64 2024 (print) | LCC QL666.L29 (ebook) | DDC 597.95/968--dc23/eng/20230803
LC record available at https://lccn.loc.gov/2023036151
LC ebook record available at https://lccn.loc.gov/2023036152

Text copyright © 2024 by Bellwether Media, Inc. BLASTOFF! READERS and associated logos are trademarks and/or registered trademarks of Bellwether Media, Inc.

Editor: Kieran Downs   Designer: Brittany McIntosh

Printed in the United States of America, North Mankato, MN.

Table of Contents

Giant Lizards	4
In Danger!	8
Save the Komodo Dragons!	12
Glossary	22
To Learn More	23
Index	24

Giant Lizards

claw

Komodo dragons are the largest lizards in the world! They have powerful tails and sharp claws.

Their long, forked tongues help them hunt **prey**.

tongue

Komodo dragons only live on a few islands in Indonesia. They are **endangered**.

People have caused most of their troubles.

Komodo Dragon Range

N W E S

range = ▢

7

In Danger!

Komodo dragons once had wider **home ranges**. But people cleared land for towns and farms. Dragon homes became smaller.

Poachers kill dragons for their body parts.

Threats

1. people need towns and farms

2. land is cleared

3. Komodo dragon homes get smaller

Komodo dragons live in low-lying grasslands. But **climate change** is causing oceans to rise.

Dragon homes could soon be under water.

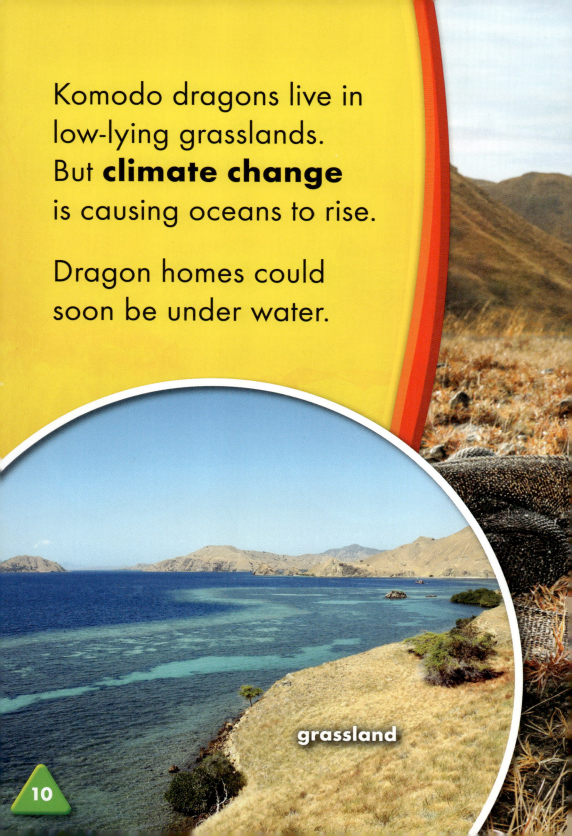

grassland

Komodo Dragon Stats

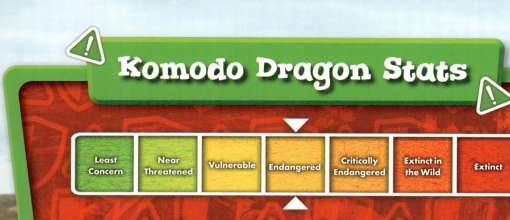

| Least Concern | Near Threatened | Vulnerable | Endangered | Critically Endangered | Extinct in the Wild | Extinct |

conservation status: endangered
life span: about 30 years

Save the Komodo Dragons!

Komodo dragons are **apex predators**. They mainly hunt animals that eat plants.

Without dragons, prey would eat more plants. Other animals would have less food.

The World with Komodo Dragons

1. more Komodo dragons

2. healthy number of prey

3. healthy number of plants

Indonesia set up a national park where Komodo dragons live. It is illegal for people to live or hunt on this land.

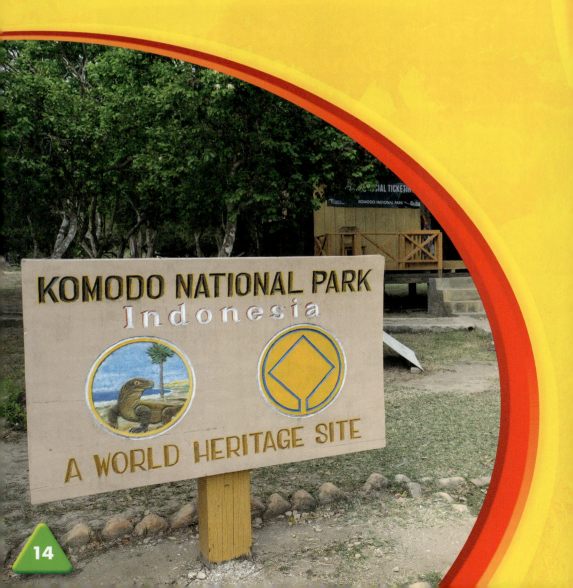

Komodo dragons have a peaceful home.

People must follow rules when visiting the park. They watch dragons from a distance.

People and Komodo dragons stay safe.

Wildlife workers closely study Komodo dragons. They find new ways to **protect** them.

Rangers patrol the park. They use **technology** to stop poachers.

Anyone can help Komodo dragons. Walking or riding bikes instead of driving slows climate change.

Donations help wildlife groups. Everyone can work together to save these giant lizards!

Glossary

apex predators—animals that are not preyed upon by other animals

climate change—a human-caused change in Earth's weather due to warming temperatures

donations—gifts for a certain cause; most donations are money.

endangered—in danger of dying out

home ranges—the lands on which groups of animals live and travel

poachers—hunters who catch or harm animals illegally

prey—animals that are hunted by other animals for food

protect—to keep safe

rangers—people in charge of protecting an area of land

technology—special tools that use scientific knowledge to make jobs easier

To Learn More

AT THE LIBRARY

Golusky, Jackie. *Komodo Dragons: Nature's Biggest Lizard.* Minneapolis, Minn.: Lerner Publications, 2024.

Kingsley, Imogen. *Komodo Dragons.* Mankato, Minn.: Amicus, 2019.

Murray, Julie. *Komodo Dragon.* Minneapolis, Minn.: ABDO, 2020.

ON THE WEB

FACTSURFER

Factsurfer.com gives you a safe, fun way to find more information.

1. Go to www.factsurfer.com.

2. Enter "Komodo dragons" into the search box and click 🔍.

3. Select your book cover to see a list of related content.

Index

apex predators, 12
claws, 4
climate change, 10, 20
donations, 20
endangered, 6
farms, 8
grasslands, 10
home ranges, 8
hunt, 5, 12, 14
Indonesia, 6, 14
national park, 14, 16, 19
oceans, 10
people, 7, 8, 14, 16, 17
plants, 12, 13
poachers, 9, 19
prey, 5, 13
range, 7
rangers, 19
rules, 16
size, 4
stats, 11
tails, 4
technology, 19

threats, 9
tongues, 5
towns, 8
ways to help, 20
wildlife groups, 20
wildlife workers, 18
world with, 13

The images in this book are reproduced through the courtesy of: GUDKOV ANDREY, front cover (Komodo dragon); Don Mammoser, front cover (tear top); Michal Szymanski, front cover (bottom tear); Eric Isselee, pp. 3, 22; Sergey Uryadnikov, pp. 4, 5, 6, 9 (bottom), 15, 20-21; Martina Pellecchia, p. 8; RossiAgung, p. 9 (top left); Rich Carey, p. 9 (top right); Takashi Images, p. 10; David Fleetham/ Alamy, pp. 10-11; CKChong, p. 12; Sony Herdiana, p. 13 (top left); Oksana Golubeva, p. 13 (top right); Tanitkji, p. 13 (bottom); Sirintra Pumsopa, p. 14; Lee Risar, p. 16; Nature Picture Library/ Alamy, p. 17; Ethan Daniels/ Alamy, p. 18; Cindy Hopkins/ Alamy, p. 19; MPH Photos, p. 20.